Death
Customs

Lucy Rushton

Wayland

Understanding Religions

Birth Customs
Death Customs
Food and Fasting
Initiation Customs
Marriage Customs
Pilgrimages and Journeys

About this book

This book looks at customs associated with death in six of the major religions of the world. The book describes ritual practices, showing how they are a context for people's feelings about death. Attitudes to death point towards people's ultimate beliefs. Looking at death customs can lead to some understanding of the faith and sense of purpose of those who take part in them.

Each chapter covers a theme associated with death across the religions so that readers may compare attitudes and beliefs. Teachers will find that elements of each chapter can be related to children's experience, whether they have encountered death directly in their own lives or not.

Editor: Joanna Housley
Designer: Malcolm Walker

This edition published in 1995 by
Wayland (Publishers) Limited

First published in 1992 by
Wayland (Publishers) Limited
61 Western Road, Hove
East Sussex, BN3 1JD, England

© Copyright 1992 Wayland (Publishers) Limited

British Library Cataloguing in Publication Data
Rushton, Lucy
    Death Customs. - (Understanding Religions Series)
    I. Title   II. Series
    291.4

HARDBACK ISBN 0-7502-0419-2

PAPERBACK ISBN 0-7502-1666-2

Typeset by Kudos Editorial and Design Services
Printed in Italy by G Canale C.S.p.A. Turin

Contents

Words that appear in **bold** in the text are explained in the glossary on page 30.

Introduction

Have you ever ridden on a fairground ghost train? Did you shiver as you went into the dark, because you did not know what would happen? Did you shudder as cobwebs trailed across your face and scream as the grinning skeleton jumped out in front of you? Is that what death is like?

When it happens to someone close, we feel death is a terrible thing, taking those we love away from us and from all that makes people happy. Yet many religions teach that complete happiness can only be found after death. They teach that even if death is like a dark tunnel, a person passes through it and comes out into sunshine again.

Above **Memorials** to the dead remind us that everyone must die.

Words and symbols

People of all **faiths** use words and **symbols** to help them understand the meaning of life and death. The words sometimes come from the holy books of each religion. Symbols are actions or objects which have a special meaning. They help us to think about things which we cannot put into words.

When we read and write about religion we have to use a word for 'God'. That word is a symbol too, because nobody can say or understand exactly what God is like. Different faiths use different words. English-speaking Christians say God. The Jewish word is Yahweh. The Muslim word is Allah. The Sikh word is Nam. Hindus call the power behind the universe Brahman.

For people who believe that death is a change, not an ending, it is a very important moment. Religious believers have many customs which they think help the dead person to pass through what they may describe as a dark tunnel. Different faiths have different ideas about what happens at the end of physical life.

Below The death of Jesus on a cross marks a beginning, for Christians, not an end.

One life?

In some religions there is a belief that the dead will rise and live again. This is called **resurrection**. Christians, Jews and Muslims believe that the dead will come back to life to be with God. In these religions there is the belief that people live once and die once.

Christians, the followers of Jesus Christ, believe Jesus showed that death is not the end of a person. He died by being crucified, which meant being nailed to a cross. He was dead for three days. But then His followers found Him alive again. They believe that Jesus rose from the dead. He promised His followers that they, too, could live for

5

ever with God. The cross Jesus died on is a symbol of hope for Christians.

Muslims believe that there will be a last day of judgement. On this day people will be raised from the dead to be judged before God. Then they will go either to paradise or to hell, depending on whether they have led a good life or a bad life. Jews also believe that, at the end of time, God will raise the dead and judge everyone. Those who have led good lives will be with God forever, and the wicked will go to hell.

Many lives?

In other religions there is the belief that a person's **soul** will come back to earth in another form and live inside another body. The belief that people live many lives, and die many deaths, is called **reincarnation**. Hindus believe that the soul has to pass through many lives before it finally becomes free. By leading

Left Mourners have to say goodbye to the person they have loved. Hindus try to accept death as a natural change.

Above The Buddha taught his followers that it is possible to escape from the endless chain of births and deaths to find peace.

a good life a person can help the soul to escape from being reborn. Then the soul returns to Brahman, the great God of the universe. Each time a person dies he or she makes a step towards this happiness.

Sikhs believe a person's soul comes from God and will go back to God if he or she leads a good life. If people are wicked they have to live again and again until they lead a good life.

Buddhists believe that, most often, part of a person goes on into another life after death. If the person has learnt to live in a truly unselfish way, then he or she reaches **nirvana**, which is a state of being where there is no longer any desire, hatred or greed.

Being ready to die

Dying means going away from what you know into something strange and unknown. People sometimes think of it as a journey. This can be frightening, but often, people who have a religious faith feel they have something to trust in, so they are not afraid.

If possible, people like to be ready for death. Christians believe that God will forgive all sins, however bad, if a person is truly sorry. This is why many Christians, especially Roman Catholics and **Orthodox Christians**, wish to confess their sins to a priest just before they die. They say sorry to God and hear the priest telling them that they are forgiven. Roman Catholics and

Sital, a Hindu boy, says:
'I remember when my grandfather had had a stroke and was going to die, they invited the family. They got a glass of holy water. Everyone took turns to put a spoonful of the water in his mouth. The holy water was from India, from the Ganges.'

Above The body of a dead Hindu is prepared for cremation and covered with a marigold-coloured cloth.

Orthodox Christians may also receive Holy Unction — when special oil is put on the dying person's forehead as medicine for the soul. This is to help the person die peacefully.

Hindus believe that the River Ganges, in India, is a holy river. They hope that their souls may not be born again into new lives. They believe that by dying near the holy river they may be saved from many rebirths. Hindus who cannot reach the holy river may be given water from the Ganges just before they die.

Death is a time to remember the most important things. Jews hope that the last words they hear are a prayer called the *Shema*:

'Hear O Israel, the Lord your God, the Lord is One. You shall love the Lord your God with all your heart, with all your soul, and with all your strength.'

The people who are with a dying Jew may encourage him or her to say sorry to God for any sins they may have committed.

A dying Muslim tries to say the *Shahadah*, a prayer which says what Muslims believe:

'There is no God but Allah, and Muhammad is His messenger.'

Sikhs think that death is like sleep. The person's soul rests for a while before going on to another life. They say the bedtime prayer, the *Sohila*, for a dead person. It is a prayer which reminds Sikhs, every day, what their life is for. It tells them that if they try to find God He will live in their hearts and they need not be afraid of dying.

Below Muslims believe they should pray five times every day. It helps them to remember God in everything they do.

Burial and cremation

Above   A Sikh funeral procession. Sikhs try to make sure that a funeral is not a gloomy occasion.

'Worn out clothes are cast off by the body. Worn out bodies are cast off by the person who lives in them.'

Hindus read this in one of their holy books, the *Gita*. When someone close to you dies, one of the saddest things is the feeling that they have gone, even though the body is still there. Something must be done with the body that has been cast off by the dead person.

Almost everywhere, people are either buried or **cremated** after death. If they

11

Left Hindus in India often choose to travel to Varanasi on the holy river Ganges before they die. Many people are cremated there and their ashes put into the river.

are buried, the body is put into a grave which may be marked in some way, often with a stone. If they are cremated, the body is burnt to ashes. In some countries this is done at a **crematorium**. In other countries the body is placed on a large pile of wood, which is set alight.

Sometimes the relatives help with the burial or cremation. This shows they accept that the person really is gone and they are willing to let them go. Jewish mourners all help to shovel earth on to the **coffin**. A Hindu's eldest son has the

Above A Buddhist funeral carriage in Thailand.

job of lighting the cremation fire.

Funerals can be very grand and showy. It is a last chance to celebrate the life of the person. Buddhist funerals are sometimes very expensive. Buddhists in Thailand use a beautifully-decorated carriage to carry the body.

Some people choose to keep things simple. Jews and Muslims try to show that everybody is equal when they are dead. They leave behind all their wealth and material importance. A dead Muslim is carefully washed and then wrapped in one or more white sheets. Muslims are taught that nobody should be buried in finer cloth than anybody else. Muslims are always buried, rather than cremated.

A Muslim grave is very plain, but it is usually raised above the ground a little.

Salam, a Muslim girl, says:
'When a Muslim is dying, he or she tries to face in the direction of **Mecca**. Muslims are buried in that direction, too. It's like when we pray to God, we turn that way. We say Mecca is the place where God lives. But really God is like light. I think He's everywhere. It's as if He is just behind you all the time!'

Orthodox Christians believe a person should be buried, not cremated. They believe that the body should be kept all in one place ready to come back to life when Jesus returns to earth. Other Christians think that people's souls will rise from the dead, even if their bodies have been cremated. At a Christian funeral service, while the body is being buried or the ashes scattered, the priest or minister will say:

'Earth to earth.
Ashes to ashes.
Dust to dust.'

This reminds people that the body is not the most important part of a person. After death it becomes no more than dust or ashes.

Orthodox Jews also choose to bury their dead. They believe that a person is made in the likeness of God and that it is wrong to destroy the body by burning. **Progressive Jews**, however, sometimes choose cremation.

Hindus are cremated. The body of the dead person is wrapped in a cloth and put on a pile of wood. Melted butter (called *ghee*) is thrown on the fire to help it burn. Three days later the ashes are gathered up. They are wrapped in a cloth and then, if possible, they are put into the holy River Ganges. Hindus living in other countries may send the ashes to India.

Above A Christian cemetery in Greece. Women visit the graves often to light candles and pray for the dead.

A new beginning

When a person you love has died, you are full of questions, like 'Where has he gone?' 'How can I talk to her now?' and 'How can I help him?'

What happens after death?
Christians say that a good person's soul 'goes to heaven' when he or she dies. They say that being in heaven means being with God. That is something Christians look forward to, even if they cannot say exactly what it will be like. Many Christians hope that in heaven they will be with their loved ones who have already died.

Christians are taught that everyone can be forgiven and can live for ever

Right   Catholics hold Masses like this one to help the dead. Christians remember that Jesus gave his life to help them when they die.

with God if they choose. But although God wants to forgive everyone, those who are separated from God, or do not believe in His forgiveness when they die, will never be close to Him after death. Roman Catholics know that most people will have done something wrong during their lives. They believe that when they die they wait for a while in a place called purgatory before reaching heaven. Relatives can help souls in purgatory by having masses said for them. Masses are church services where bread and wine are shared.

Hindus believe that a person's soul has to live many lives before it can go back to Brahman. They are taught that those who lead good lives climb a little higher up a kind of ladder. At the bottom of the ladder are simple creatures, such as insects and reptiles. After many lives a soul is born into a human. Some human souls are nearer the top of the ladder than others. The group of people called Brahmins are nearest the top. When Brahmins die, their souls are most likely to go back to Brahman.

Like Hindus, Sikhs believe that a person's soul is a little separate part of God (Nam), which will be joined up with Him again. But they do not think that some are higher up the ladder than others. By leading a good life, anybody can get close to God again. Sikh customs

Above Many Hindus believe that Brahmins are the group of people closest to Brahman. They are expected to pray more often than other Hindus and to perform many rituals. Bathing in the river is a symbol for being pure.

show they believe that everybody is equal. For example, they all share food together at the **gurdwara**.

Buddhist teaching says that people do not have individual souls. The Buddha explained that a person is like a stream of water flowing along. Most of the stream stops flowing when a person dies, but part of the stream (or force) goes into another life. This force is called karma. Buddhists believe that if they follow the teaching of the Buddha they can stop the karma from going on into another life. That means they reach nirvana, which is a final state of being, when a person has no selfish desires.

Right Buddhists believe that unless a person learns how to escape, one life follows another like the turning of a wheel. This Tibetan wall painting shows the Buddhist Wheel of Life.

Judgement

Crash! A supermarket trolley swings round the corner too fast. It hits a stack of baked beans. The tins tumble down and roll away. Somebody steps on one and falls on to a shelf of bottles. Just imagine the scene. People are shouting, babies are crying and there is fruit juice all over the floor. Every action has results — sometimes a chain of results like this. Remembering this makes us thoughtful about what we do.

Many people who follow a religious path are taught that what they do matters very much indeed. They know that they can choose to help others or hurt them. They also believe their choices have consequences which will affect what happens to them when they die.

Hindus and Buddhists believe the way they live affects them in future lives. Muslims, Sikhs, Christians and Jews feel that God sees everything they do. They believe He will judge them after they die to decide whether they should be punished or rewarded.

Jews believe that the Messiah, a great leader, will come and make the world a better place. Then there will be the Day of Judgement. Because they expect the coming of the Messiah, Jews think about

Above Buddhist memorials like these symbolize reaching the point of nirvana when greed and hate disappear.

how to make the world better. Because they expect God to judge them, they think about how they should behave. When a Jew is about to die, the people who are there say *'Blessed be the truthful judge'*, because they trust God to be fair.

Jews believe they have been told how to live their lives. Their holy books give many careful instructions, including telling them how to cut their hair and cook their food. If they are used to obeying God's teachings they will find it easy to lead good lives. Orthodox Jews try to stick closely to these practices. Progressive Jews feel that the teachings can be adapted to make them more

Below The Torah is the most important of Jewish holy books. Scrolls like this are carefully kept in every synagogue and read at all services.

relevant to modern lifestyles.

Muslims expect to be judged on a Day of Judgement. They believe the Angel of Death will blow a trumpet and all the dead will have to cross a narrow bridge over hell. The wicked will fall in and the good ones reach paradise. Muslims believe that God is always fair. When it seems unfair that a good person suffers during life, they remember that he or she will be rewarded after death. They also believe God is merciful and will forgive those who are really sorry for any wrong they have done. The funeral prayer asks for forgiveness for the living and the dead.

Sikhs believe that a person has more than one chance to live a good life. A bad person's soul is born into another life. A good person goes to join God.

Hindus and Buddhists believe that their actions have effects which go on after they die. In Buddhism this is called the law of karma. No one can escape the law of karma. The Buddha taught:

'If a man speaks or acts with an evil thought, pain follows him as the wheel follows the foot of the ox that draws the wagon.'

Hindus and Buddhists believe that if they do wrong they cannot escape from being born again. Hindus hope to make progress towards *moksha*, which means being joined to Brahman: leading a bad

Right Monks lead a funeral procession in Thailand. Some Buddhists feel that ordinary people have little chance of escaping rebirth. They have to hope to become monks or nuns in a future life.

life means taking a backward step. Buddhists hope to reach the final blissful state of nirvana: a bad life means they have wasted the chance. Both Hindus and Buddhists believe that evil deeds lead to suffering in future lives.

Mourning

Traditional customs help people to know what to do when someone dies. These customs may help them to feel better about that person's death by letting them express their feelings and think about their religious hopes for that person.

There is a tradition in some Jewish families when someone dies, that the closest relatives will stay in the house sitting on low stools. Neighbours and friends will come to comfort them, and bring meals and other practical help.

Below Orthodox Jews remembering a relative in Jerusalem.

Jeremie, a Jewish boy, says:

'When my uncle died two years ago, all the family helped my aunt and cousins. At the funeral, most people threw some earth on top of the coffin. I remember everyone saying the *kaddish*. They still say it once a year on the day that he died.'

This is because the close relatives are not expected to do any ordinary tasks when a member of their family has died.

Muslims try to trust God all their lives. They know they should trust Him when someone they love has died, but it is difficult not to be sad. When a member of a Muslim family has died, the mourners do not cook for themselves for forty days. Relatives and neighbours bring food. When the forty days are over the family invite all relatives and friends to a meal. Sometimes they cook the dead person's seven favourite foods and serve a little to each guest.

Signs of mourning

Jews make a tear in their clothes as soon as someone close to them has died. For the first week they do not eat meat or drink wine. They should not go to work, listen to music or read the Torah. For the first month after a relative has died they should not cut their hair or shave, or wear new clothes. They believe that God shares in their suffering and helps them to bear it. They say parts of a prayer called the *kaddish*. These rituals can help mourners to come to terms with their loss and grief.

When a Hindu has died, the family makes offerings of rice balls and milk (*pinda*) for the dead person at a shrine, every day for ten days. Relatives and friends join the family for the cremation. They come again on the fourth and eleventh days to share the family's grief. They all offer rice balls and milk. They believe this helps the soul to move on to its next life. It is a last chance for friends and relatives to give the dead person a gift.

Sikhs do not make a great show of grief because they believe dying and being reborn helps people on their way back to God. So at the moment when someone dies they shout *'Waheguru'*, which means *'Wonderful Lord!'* Relatives and friends gather at the house to see the body. They take gifts of money and oil. The body is taken in a coffin to the gurdwara. Then there is the cremation, followed by another service back at the gurdwara. Like all Sikh services, this ends with the sharing of **kara parshad** and other food. During the days and nights after the funeral, all the adults of the family take part in reading the whole of the Guru Granth Sahib (the Sikh holy book). This may take at least two days.

A Buddhist funeral may sometimes look like a joyful occasion, with music and a feast and even fireworks. Buddhists try to learn not to be afraid of death. Monks come to the funeral and recite the most important prayers of Buddhism. The first prayer is called the Three Jewels. It reminds Buddhists of

Above At a Hindu cremation the body is burnt in a stack of wood.

the three things they trust in - the Buddha, the Dharma (the way of life which the Buddha taught), and the Sangha (the monks who follow that way of life). The monks and people also say the Five Precepts, which are rules for living a good life. The time when someone dies can be a good moment for those who are left to think about how they should be living their lives.

Right A beautifully-decorated Buddhist cremation tower. The whole tower will be burnt with the body.

Remembering

The first reaction many people have to the death of someone close to them is to be sad. But then people also remember what the dead person was like, and what he or she did for them. In some religions there are customs associated with remembering, to show that a person who has died is still in people's thoughts.

When Orthodox Christians hold a service in memory of someone who has died, they invite people by giving them

Below In a Christian churchyard, stones and crosses mark the graves where people are buried. The names on the stones remind Christians of loved ones who have died.

Above Muslims may read their holy book, the Qur'an, from beginning to end as a gift to a relative who has died.

a loaf of bread. At the service a special kind of porridge is given to the mourners. The porridge is made of grains of wheat. This symbolizes new life, because the wheat is soft and damp, like seeds in the spring before they sprout. Each person takes a little of the mixture and says, *'May God forgive'*. They believe that giving away food helps the soul of the dead person. While a person is alive, he or she needs food for the body. Once the soul has left the body, it leaves behind the things the body needed. The soul goes on to a new spiritual life.

Some Orthodox Christians take the body out of the grave, after a number of years and wash the bones with wine before putting them in a box in a special building. They believe that when the bones are clean the soul is free of sins. The mourners feel their loved one can now be happy.

Jews feel it is a duty to remember a relative who has died. Each year, on the day of the death, close relatives light a candle which burns for twenty-four hours. They usually say the *kaddish* prayer again.

Muslims read the Qur'an (the Muslim holy book) right through as a gift to the dead. The members of a family share parts of it out and read it as many times as they can between them. They do this for forty days after someone has died, and again each year on the anniversary of the person's death. Sometimes relatives light candles and **incense** sticks on the grave or sprinkle sugary water.

Signs of remembering

Sometimes people want to feel that some sign of their loved one's life will last for a long time. When Jews, Muslims and Christians are buried, it is usual to mark the grave with a stone. The person's name is carved on the stone. A stone

Matthew, age 9, says: 'My family are Christians. My elder brother died last year, and he is buried here in the graveyard of our church. Every week one of the family comes here to keep the grave tidy, and water the flowers, to show that he is not forgotten.'

memorial lasts for centuries. Sometimes Christian memorials are very grand. Jews and Muslims believe they should be kept simple.

People often offer candles or flowers as gifts for the dead. They are beautiful but they do not last long. They remind mourners that all life has to end.

Right Flowers are gifts for the dead in this Spanish cemetery.

Glossary

Coffin A box in which a dead body is buried or cremated.

Cremate To burn a body to ashes.

Crematorium A building in which bodies are cremated.

Faiths Specific systems of religious beliefs.

Gurdwara A Sikh place of worship.

Incense A substance that is burnt to produce a sweet smell.

Kaddish An ancient Jewish prayer that mourners say at a funeral, and on the anniversary of a death.

Kara parshad A dish made from flour, sugar and butter, which Sikhs eat together in their temples.

Mecca The holiest city for Muslims, where the prophet Muhammad was born.

Memorial Something (such as a building or gravestone) which is built to show that someone who has died is not forgotten.

Nirvana In Buddhism, the final release from being reborn over and over again. This is reached when a person no longer has any selfish desires.

Orthodox Christians Members of the division of the Christian church based mainly in Eastern Europe.

Orthodox Jews Jews who strictly follow the teachings God revealed to the prophet, Moses.

Progressive Jews Jews who believe that the teachings of Moses can be adapted for the modern world.

Reincarnation The belief that on the death of the body the soul is born again in another body.

Resurrection The belief that dead people return to life.

Soul The spirit of a person, that some people believe survives the body after death.

Symbol Something that represents or stands for something else.

Further information

Books to read

The following series contain useful information about the religions dealt with in this book:

Looking into World Religions (Batsford, 1989)

My Belief (Franklin Watts, 1989)

Our Culture (Franklin Watts, 1989)

Religion Around Us (Oliver & Boyd, 1990)

Religions of the World (Simon & Schuster, 1992)

Religions of the World (Wayland, 1986)

Religious Topics (Wayland, 1987)

Classroom materials:

A Gift to the Child   Religious Education in the Early Years Project, University of Birmingham, School of Education (Simon & Schuster, 1991) This useful pack contains a teachers' source book, pupils' books and a cassette.

Picture acknowledgements

The publishers wish to thank the following for supplying the photographs in this book: J Allan Cash 4, 7, 11, 12, 18, 29; Cephas Picture Library 9 (Nigel Blythe); Eye Ubiquitous 8 (VC Sievey); Sonia Halliday 5, 10 (Jane Taylor), 15, 22 (Jane Taylor), 26, 27; Hutchison Picture Library 13 (top, Trevor Page), 16, 17, 19 (Liba Taylor), 21 (Jeremy Horner), 23, 25 (R Ian Lloyd); Ann and Bury Peerless 24; Lucy Rushton 14; Wayland Picture Library 13 (bottom), 28 (David Cumming); ZEFA 6.

Index

Numbers in **bold** indicate photographs